Evelyn
Tourettes Syndrome
Awareness

Printed in USA

Three Clever Chickies Publishing Co.
8876 Vintage Park Drive
Sacramento, CA 96828

threecleverchickiespublishingco.com

THREE CLEVER CHICKIES PUBLISHING CO.

Dedicated to my son,
Zaden, who has a heart of gold.
He continues to remind me to never
let obstacles in life define who you are.
He gracefully embraced Tourette's Syndrome
and continues to spread awareness.

My name is Zee,
I am six.

Today I want to talk
about my tics.

No, I'm not talking about those little bugs.

Not the ones that you may find crawling on the rugs.

The fancy name is Tourette's.
You may wonder...why?
It was named after Georges Tourette,
who first described his behaviors in 1885.

Tics are movements and
sounds that I cannot control.
Teaching you all about my tics;
that's my goal.

You may ask,
"What kind of sounds do you make?"
I make different sounds,
sometimes hissing like a snake.

A B C D E F G H I J K L M N O P Q R S T U V W X Y Z
What is Tourettes Syndrome?
What are tics?

I also make movements
like quick eye blinks.
It sometimes makes me worry
about what everyone thinks.

Sometimes it's constant
throat clearing;
Or making faces,
I promise I am not sneering.

Most of all, I tend to squeak.
I try my best to hold it in
when I speak.

Blink!
Ahem!
Squeak!

I will not squeak today.
I will not squeak today.
I will not squeak today.

SQUEAK!
AHEM!
AHEM!
SQUEAK!
SQUEAK!

Being worried can make
my tics worse.
I try my best to stop it,
I even rehearse.

But you see,
it's impossible even if I try my best.
You may see my tics getting worse
when I'm taking a test.

My tics also worsen when
I am ill, stressed, excited or tired.

I know this is a lot to learn about me,
but that's just how I am wired.

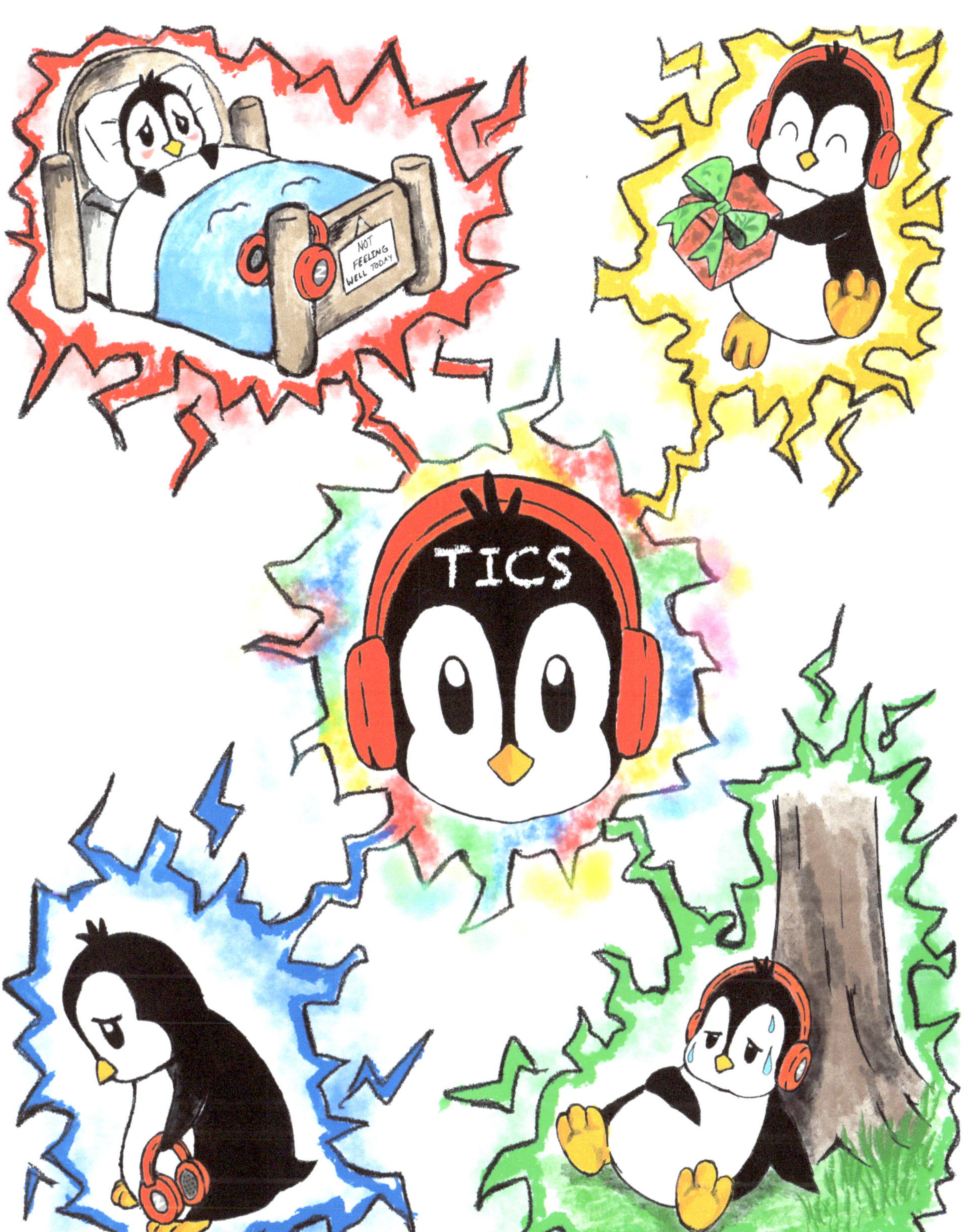
NOT FEELING WELL TODAY
TICS

To my teacher,
please be patient with me.

My tics may look like
I’m shaking my head “no,”
but really I agree.

Mrs. B
Zee
Paco
Pao
Pop Quiz
3 + 2 =
3 - 3 =
3 + 4 =

Mrs. B, please don't
put me on timeout if I make
noises during quiet time.

I’m really trying,
and having tics isn’t a crime.

ZEE

I am different,
but I am more like you than you know.
I like video games,
pizza and the snow.

If you just get to know me you will see.
I am fun and you might really like me.

Tourettes Awareness

Remember, his and her tics
may be different from mine.

Please be a patient friend
and we will be just fine.

The End

www.ingramcontent.com/pod-product-compliance
Lightning Source LLC
LaVergne TN
LVHW071240210926
848486LV00007B/309